Fact Finders®

MEDIA LITERACY

At The Controls

Questioning Video and Computer Games

by Neil Andersen

Capstone *press*®

Mankato, Minnesota

Fact Finders is published by Capstone Press,
151 Good Counsel Drive, P.O. Box 669, Mankato, Minnesota 56002.
www.capstonepress.com

Library of Congress Cataloging-in-Publication Data
Andersen, Neil.
  At the controls : questioning video and computer games / by Neil Andersen.
    p. cm.—(Fact finders. Media literacy)
  Summary: "Describes what media is, how video and computer games are a part of media, and encourages readers to question the medium's influential messages"—Provided by publisher.
  Includes bibliographical references and index.
  ISBN-13: 978-0-7368-6768-9 (hardcover)
  ISBN-10: 0-7368-6768-6 (hardcover)
  ISBN-13: 978-0-7368-7864-7 (softcover pbk.)
  ISBN-10: 0-7368-7864-5 (softcover pbk.)
  1. Video games—Juvenile literature. 2. Computer games—Juvenile literature. I. Title.
II. Series.
GV1469.3.A766 2007
794.8—dc22   2006026345

Editorial Credits
Jennifer Besel, editor; Juliette Peters, designer; Jo Miller, photo researcher/photo editor

Photo Credits
Capstone Press/Karon Dubke, 4 (all), 6 (all), 7 (all), 8, 9 (all), 10 (all), 11 (all), 12, 13 (all), 14, 15, 16, 17, 18 (all), 19, 20, 21, 22 (all), 23 (*Madden 06, Tiger Woods, X-Men*), 24, 25 (all), 27 (Xbox, *Halo 2*), 29 (*American Wasteland*)
Courtesy of the Computer History Museum, 28 (all)
Courtesy of Neil Andersen, 32
FreeCovers.net, 23 (*Greg Hastings, Gretzky, Pirates*), 26, 27 (*Greg Hastings, X-Men*), 29 (*Tiger Woods*)
Shutterstock/David Hsu, cover (controller); Duasbaew Alisher, cover (TV)

TABLE OF CONTENTS

Media Play

Did you know that right now you're holding a part of the **media**? Don't put it down. It's trying to tell you something. That's what the media does. It tries to communicate messages. Books are only one part of the media. Movies, TV shows, and even video games are part of the media too.

We are around the media all day. And we get a lot of our information and entertainment from it. Because we rely on media so much, it has the power to **influence** us. Asking questions about what we see and hear is a good way to understand media messages. Let's try it on video games.

QUESTION IT!

Who made the message and why?

Who is the message for?

How might others view the message differently?

What is left out of the message?

How does the message get and keep my attention?

Who made the message and why?

Video games are a hot business. Companies spend millions of dollars developing games. Yes, some games tank. And that can be disastrous. If a company doesn't see profits when the game comes out, the company could go broke. But for many companies, making games is worth the risk. When a game becomes a megahit, the company stands to make a ton of money.

These games are very different from each other. But they do have one thing in common. They all made their companies a lot of money.

Games are fun. Some are even educational. But remember, those aren't the only reasons games are made.

And money—well, that's what it's all about. Gaming companies make games to make money. Sure, games are cool and very entertaining. But companies work hard to make them that way so we'll buy or download them.

Ads on Your Memory Card

Selling games isn't the only way companies make money. Some games include product placements right in the scenes. Play *Sims Online* and you'll see products and logos from Intel and McDonald's. These companies paid a hefty sum to be featured in the game. But why? Companies want you to be familiar with their name, logo, and products. Being part of a game is just another way to **advertise**.

LINGO

product placement: putting products and logos in games so players will see them

Some people say product placements make games feel more like real life. What do you think?

Reality Check

In 2005, Activision released the Tony Hawk game, *American Wasteland*. It is reported that it cost the company $20 million to make that game. But Activision didn't rely on just sales to make up that cost. Product placements are all over the place in *American Wasteland*. You'll find placements for Jeep, Jeep Wrangler, Liberty, Nokia, and Motorola. Activision made $2 million just by selling ad space in the game. Next time you play, see if you can find other product placements.

Making video and computer games takes a lot of time and a lot of talent. Here are just a few of the people who work to make the games you play.

The **PRODUCER** manages the budget, the schedule, and the development of a game.

GAME DESIGNERS plan out how the game will look and play.

A **SCRIPTER** writes what the characters will say or what we'll read on the screen.

The **GAME ARTIST** creates all the art that players see.

A **PROGRAMMER** writes the code that makes the game playable.

The **TESTER** plays the game and tells programmers about problems in the game.

Who is the message for?

Game makers know that not every player will like every game. So they make games that will appeal to a specific target audience. What does that mean? Well, companies do research to figure out who's buying their games. Did you know that the average age of gamers is 30? Gaming companies know. So they make a lot of games for that older audience.

Control the Features

Companies need to figure out what their target audience wants. Some companies set up discussion boards on their Web sites. Players talk about what they like or don't like about a game.

LINGO

target audience: the group of people that game makers think will be interested in a game's message

Another way companies get info is to send out a beta version of a game to fans. Fans play the game then report back to the company with what they liked and didn't like. If a company gets a lot of bad comments, they just might redo parts of the game.

TRY IT OUT!

A new gaming company thinks women ages 25 to 35 are a good target audience. They want you to develop a new game for women.

- First, do a little research. Ask some women who are between 25 and 35 years old what they would like in a game.
- Use what you learn to write up a summary of your new game. Include what the game would be about and what the characters would do.
- When you're done, ask some women in your target audience what they think. Do they like your idea? Why or why not?

Playable Values

How might others view the message differently?

Not everybody likes the same games. Duh! But why is that so? It's because of values. Our values, or what we believe is important or true, affect how we think and feel about a game. Our age, gender, life experiences, and religious beliefs all help us form our values. We just have to keep in mind that everybody's values are different. You might think *Grand Theft Auto* is just fun. But someone else might think it teaches people that crime is fine.

Many games use crime and violence as part of their story. Do you think playing violent games influences you to act a certain way?

Hosting a Value

Video and computer games have values in them too. And these values have a way of influencing us sometimes. **Stereotypes** are one kind of value that games **promote**. A lot of games show African Americans as athletes, but nothing else. Are black people only good at playing sports? Of course not. But if you never questioned the values in games, you just might begin to think so.

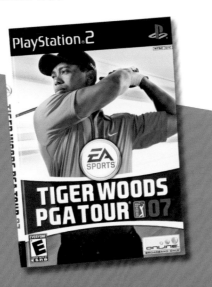

TRY IT OUT!

The people who make games have their own values. Sometimes they put those values into the games they work on. You can try doing this too.

Make up an idea for a video game that promotes one or more of your values. Here are some questions to help you decide what to promote.

- What do you love?
- What do you hate?
- What do you believe in?

You could suggest an idea for a game that promotes good sportsmanship or hard work, if those things are important to you.

Make sure you explain what kinds of words or actions the characters would say or do to promote your values.

Gender Mode

Next time you're gaming, take a quick head count. See any women? Men far outnumber women in games. What's that about? Are games sending the message that women can't do the same things as men?

And then when you do see a woman, is she wearing many clothes? Women wearing skimpy clothes sends a message. And if we don't question that message, we might begin to think that all women should dress like that.

Women in many games, like *Grand Theft Auto: San Andreas*, don't look like women in the real world. But do you think game women could influence the way you think?

Reality Check

In 1999, two high school students killed 13 people, wounded 23 others, and then shot themselves during an attack on Columbine High School. The shooters were known to be players of the first-person shooter games *Doom* and *Duke Nukem*. The families of those who were killed filed a lawsuit in 2001 against the makers of these violent games. They said the values in the games influenced the shooters to kill.

Other people disagree with this. They say games don't influence people to be violent. What do you think?

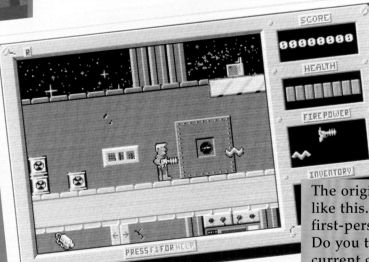

The original *Duke Nukem* looked like this. It doesn't look much like first-person shooter games today. Do you think older games and current games have the same influence on players?

Make-Believe Story Mode

What is left out of the message?

Video and computer games create a whole other world for gamers. Characters, like those in *Final Fantasy X*, look almost like real people. Characters in *Tony Hawk's Underground* skate and do tricks like skaters in real life. But games aren't exactly like the world we live in. In a game, you don't have to deal with **consequences**.

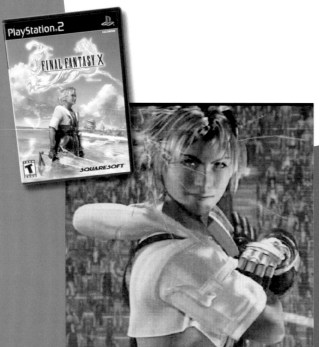

Characters and actions in games look pretty real. Do you think gamers sometimes think things in games actually are real?

Designers want to make their games as exciting and as entertaining as possible. They know gamers won't play a game that makes them clean up the mess after a high-speed chase. They leave the boring parts out.

Nope. No clean-up crew here.

Many video games try to be as real-life as possible. But they leave some things out. Well, here's your chance to make those video games really real. Make a list of things that you do each day that you rarely see in a game. Need an example? You hardly ever see characters having lunch or washing their hands.

When you're done, answer these questions.

- If a company put the things on your list in a game, would the game be very exciting? Why or why not?
- Would people buy a game that had day-to-day actions in it? Why or why not?

Abilities

A lot of violent games play tricks with reality. Game characters can often survive all kinds of attacks. Take a look at *Serious Sam*. Players get to shoot at and kill enemies. But the player's character can survive unreal amounts of damage. Games like this leave out that a real person would never live through all the violence.

We all know games are make-believe. But if we don't question what we see, we just might start to forget how much violence hurts.

Loading Action

Many games also leave out the fact that causing damage to property or to other people has an effect. Characters never have to pay for the property they destroy or comfort the family of the person they killed.

Games like *Grand Theft Auto* rarely show troublemakers getting caught. Crime might seem fun in a game, but it doesn't show you what it's like to do the time for the crime.

The high-speed chase may look fun. But if that happened in real life, what would the consequences be?

Create a Trick

How does the message get and keep my attention?

In order for us to buy the game, we have to know about it. So companies use all kinds of tricks to get our attention.

Just like movies, games are promoted using trailers. These commercials play on TV, showing the most thrilling parts of the game. The quick cuts from one scene to the next boost the jolts per minute.

Game trailers, like this one for *Lost Planet*, jump from scene to scene to get you excited to play the game.

LINGO

quick cuts: fast scene changes that are meant to jolt and excite you

jolts per minute: JPMs are fast, exciting quick cuts or action sequences that get you excited

Many games are created to go along with a movie. Companies hope games like *Pirates of the Caribbean: The Legend of Jack Sparrow* and *X-Men: The Official Game* will be big sellers because the audience liked the movies.

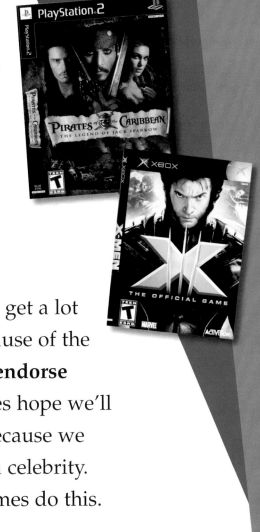

Other games get a lot of attention because of the celebrities who **endorse** them. Companies hope we'll buy the game because we want to be like a celebrity. Many sports games do this.

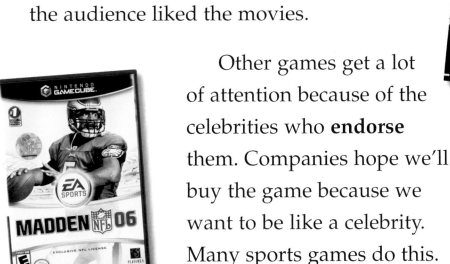

Once they get your attention, games have to keep it. Game makers have a few tricks up their sleeves to do just that.

Mods

Mods are a fun feature that lets gamers have a hand in how the game is played. Mods allow gamers to change parts of the game. And they keep you playing long after you've finished the regular game.

Some mods allow for major game changes. *Counter Strike* is a total conversion mod of the game *Half-Life*.

Options, Options, Options

A game would be boring if there weren't any options. So most games let you choose everything from the characters' clothing to the point of view. Once you play the game one way, you can change it all up and play it again.

Tony Hawk's Underground **has all kinds of options. You can even make your own skater.**

LINGO

point of view: the angle at which you see the action of the game; first-person shooter games let you see the action like you are the one holding the gun.

Diablo II **has an Easter egg called the Secret Cow Level. Yes, some hidden elements have very little to do with the rest of the game.**

Easter Eggs

Ok, so they're not really eggs, but they're still fun to find! Easter eggs add a hidden element to a game. Sometimes they are hidden rooms, sometimes whole other levels. They are there to keep you looking for more.

⚡ Reality Check

Some Easter eggs are fun to find, but have nothing to do with the game at all. On the original printing of *Tiger Woods 99 PGA Tour Golf* for PlayStation, there was an unusual Easter egg. If you popped the disc into your CD Rom and located the file marked Zzdummy.dat you would stumble across five minutes of a *South Park* episode. The problem was that no one had gotten permission to use the episode. EA Sports, the company that made the disc, didn't know it had been put on there (probably by one of the employees who worked on the game). About 100,000 copies of the disc were sold before EA reprinted the disc without the show.

Game Over

Gaming is great fun. There's no doubt about that. What's tricky, though, is the messages games send. Game messages can be very influential. But we don't have to believe everything we see when we play. That's what's so cool about the fantasy world of gaming. So grab your controller, load your game, and have fun questioning the world in your system.

Time Line

Steve Russell develops the first interactive computer game called *Spacewar*.

Nintendo begins selling its NES (Nintendo Entertainment System).

1961　　**1972**　　**1986**　　**1995**

Magnavox releases the first home video game console.

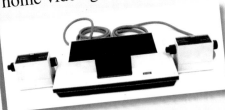

Sony begins selling the PlayStation in the United States.

Tiger Woods 99 PGA Tour Golf is released with an unauthorized Easter egg.

Activision sells $2 million worth of product placement ads in *Tony Hawk's American Wasteland*.

1999   **2001**   **2005**

Microsoft launches the Xbox.

The families of those killed in the Columbine school shooting file a lawsuit against makers of violent games.

GLOSSARY

advertise (AD-ver-tize)—to give information about something you want to sell

consequence (KON-suh-kwenss)—the result of an action

endorse (en-DORSS)—to sponsor a product by appearing in advertisements or on the product

influence (IN-floo-uhnss)—to have an effect on someone or something

media (MEE-dee-uh)—a group of mediums that communicates messages; one piece of the media, like video or computer games, is called a medium.

promote (pruh-MOTE)—to make the public aware of something or someone

stereotype (STER-ee-oh-tipe)—an overly simple opinion of a person, group, or thing

INTERNET SITES

FactHound offers a safe, fun way to find Internet sites related to this book. All of the sites on FactHound have been researched by our staff.

Here's how:

1. Visit *www.facthound.com*

2. Choose your grade level.

3. Type in this book ID **0736867686** for age-appropriate sites. You may also browse subjects by clicking on letters, or by clicking on pictures and words.

4. Click on the **Fetch It** button.

FactHound will fetch the best sites for you!

READ MORE

Ali, Dominic. *Media Madness: An Insider's Guide to Media*. Tonawanda, N.Y.: Kids Can Press, 2005.

Gedatus, Gus. *Violence in the Media*. Perspectives on Violence. Mankato, Minn.: Capstone Press, 2000.

Oleksy, Walter G. *Video Game Designer*. Coolcareers.com. New York: Rosen, 2000.

INDEX

MEET THE AUTHOR

Neil Andersen's interest in the media has led him to a career teaching others about it. Neil is an executive member of the Association for Media Literacy and serves on the board of the Media-Awareness Network. In addition to working as the media literacy consultant for the Toronto District School Board, he gives presentations and workshops worldwide.